Horse Sense
of the Carolinas, Inc

6919 Meadows Town Road
Marshall, NC 28753
828-683-7304
www.horsesenseotc.com

How sweet it is when the strong are also gentle! (Libbie Fudim)

An ounce of
behavior is
worth a pound
of words

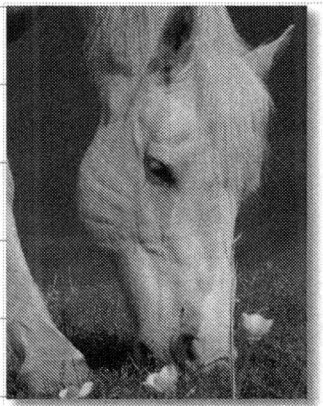

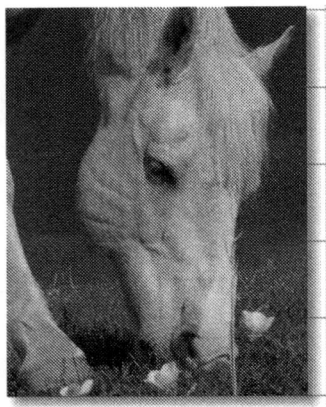

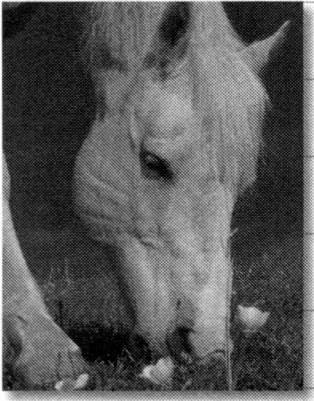

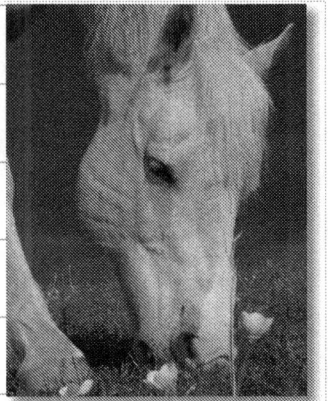

To be loved by a horse, or by any animal, should
fill us with awe--for we have not deserved it.
(Marion Garretty)

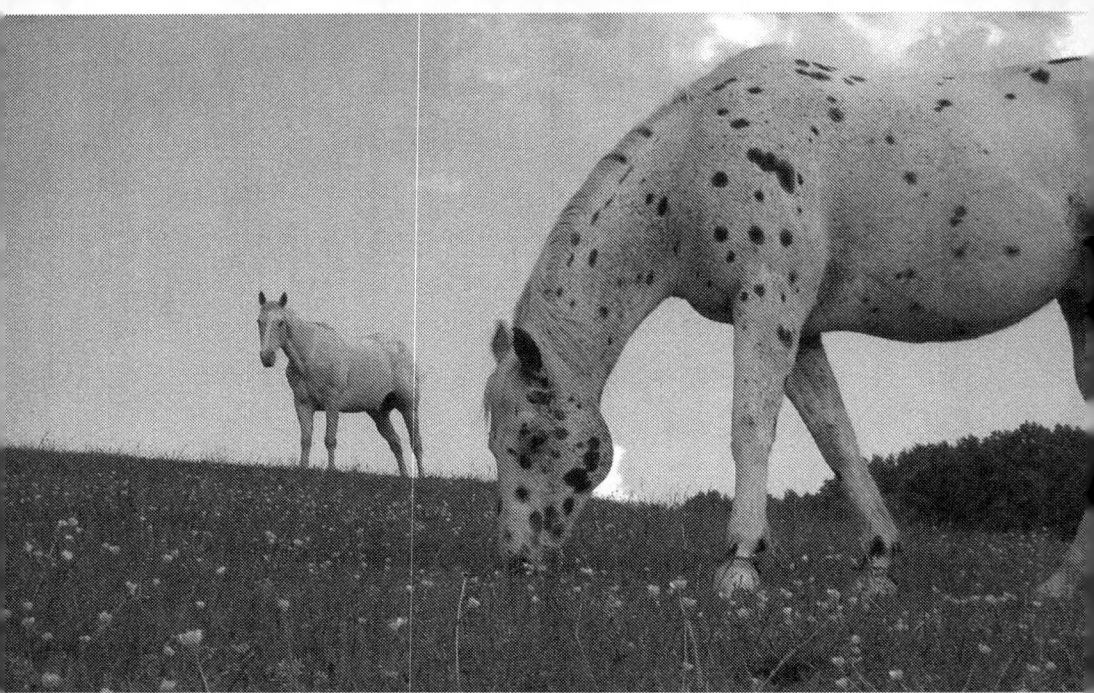

You cannot train a horse with shouts and expect it to obey a whisper (Dagobert D. Runes)

What we love, we shall grow to resemble (Bernard of Clairvaux)

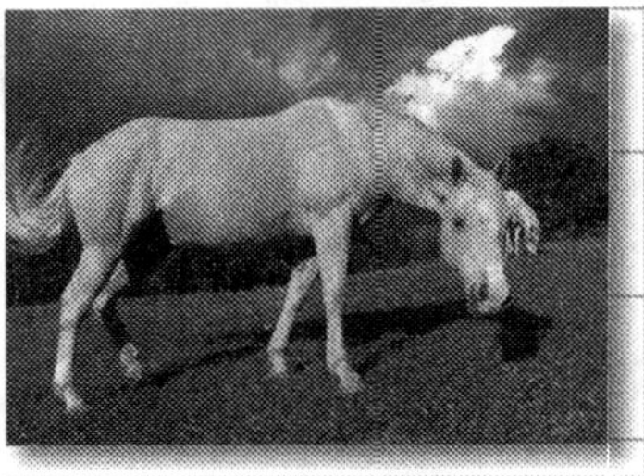

Fear almost
always arises--in
horses as well as
in people--from
concern about
what might
happen, and much
more rarely from
what IS happening
(Mary Wanless)

Not the fastest horse can catch a word spoken in anger (Chinese Proverb)

Greatness lies not
in being strong,
but in the right
use of strength
(Henry Ward
Beecher)

It is the very
difficult horses
that have
the most to
give you.
(Lendon Gray)

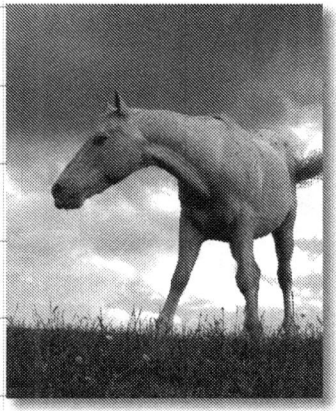

Stable thinking is the ability to say "neigh" (source unknown)

It's what you learn after you know it all that's important (Jimmy Williams)

Show me your horse and I will tell you who you are (English Proverb)

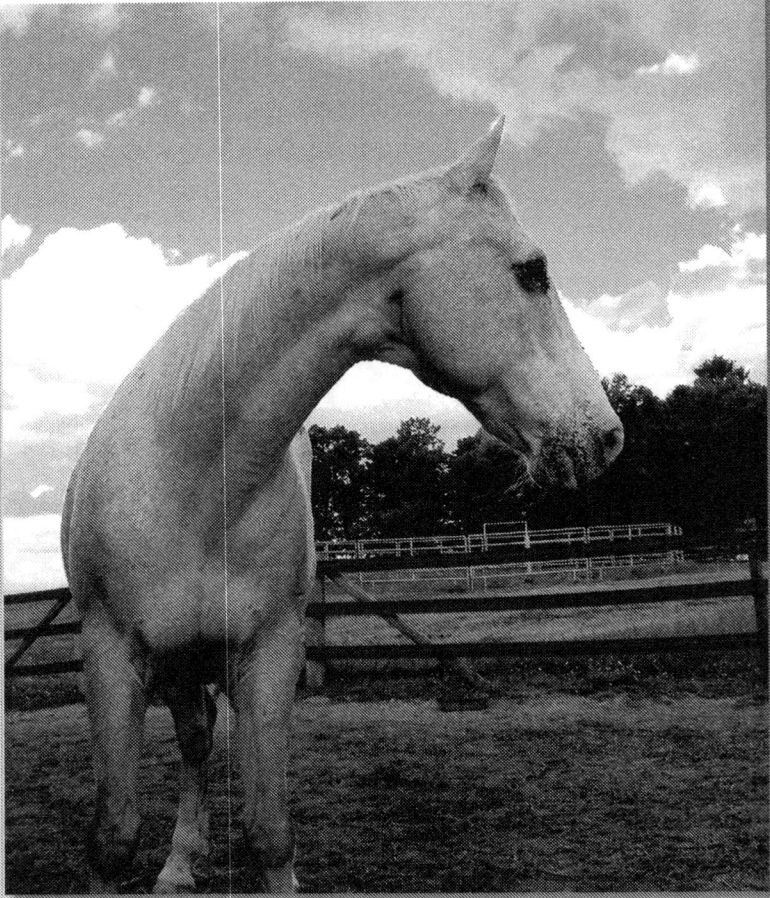

Never approach a bull from the front, a horse
from the rear or a fool from any direction
(Cowboy Saying)

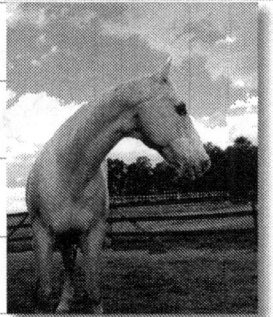

Questions to ask about your session

When the horse(s) got back to the pasture, what did he or she tell the other horses about your session?

What would you like to change in the activity?

How might the horse(s) you worked with describe you to other horses?

What did you learn about yourself?

When was the horse right-brained (reacting)? What did that look like? Why do you think the horse acted that way?

How did you read the horse's body language? How did the horse read your body language?

When was the horse left-brained (thinking)? What did that look like? Why do you think the horse acted that ways?

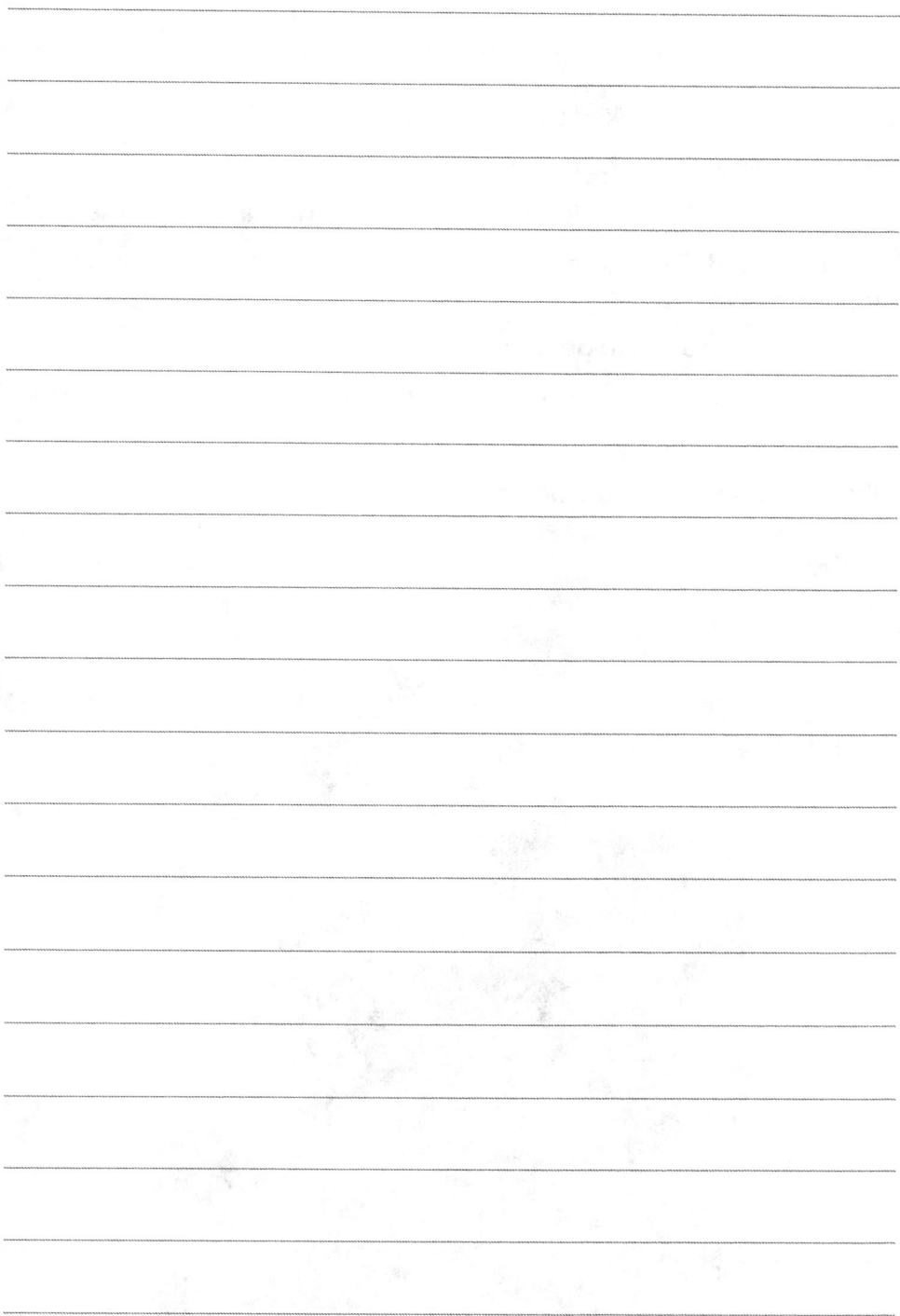

More questions to ask about your session

Who would you have liked to have in the session with you?

What happened from the horse's point of view?

Which horses did you work with and what did you learn about them?

What feelings did you have before the activity? During the activity? After the activity?

Where would you like to go from here?

How did the horse act like a prey animal? How did you act like a predator?

How did the horse(s) feel about the session?

What questions would the horse have for you?

Make it Up!

Describe a day in the life of a horse.

You are asked to a catch a wild horse and teach it how to get along in Humanville. How would you do it? What does living in Humanville mean?

Imagine you are a horse. Describe yourself as that horse: what's your name? How old are you? What color? Where do you live? What is your herd like? Do you have a person? What is that person like?

Design your own equine session activity. Write out how it would work, what you would have to do to set it up, and how many horses you would need. Think about safety as you plan.

Pick a horse from the herd. Tell his or her story, including where he/she was born, what her mom and dad were like, where she was raised, what the herd was like, and how she came to be where he or she is.

When It's Not Going Well
Questions to ask yourself:

If the problem disappeared overnight, by magic, what would your next session be like?

How come things weren't worse?

What were you doing to keep the situation from getting worse?

Write about a time when difficulty started, but you stopped it before it went any further.

How did you know to stop it before it got much worse?

What did you do that stopped it?

When things weren't going wrong, what was happening instead?

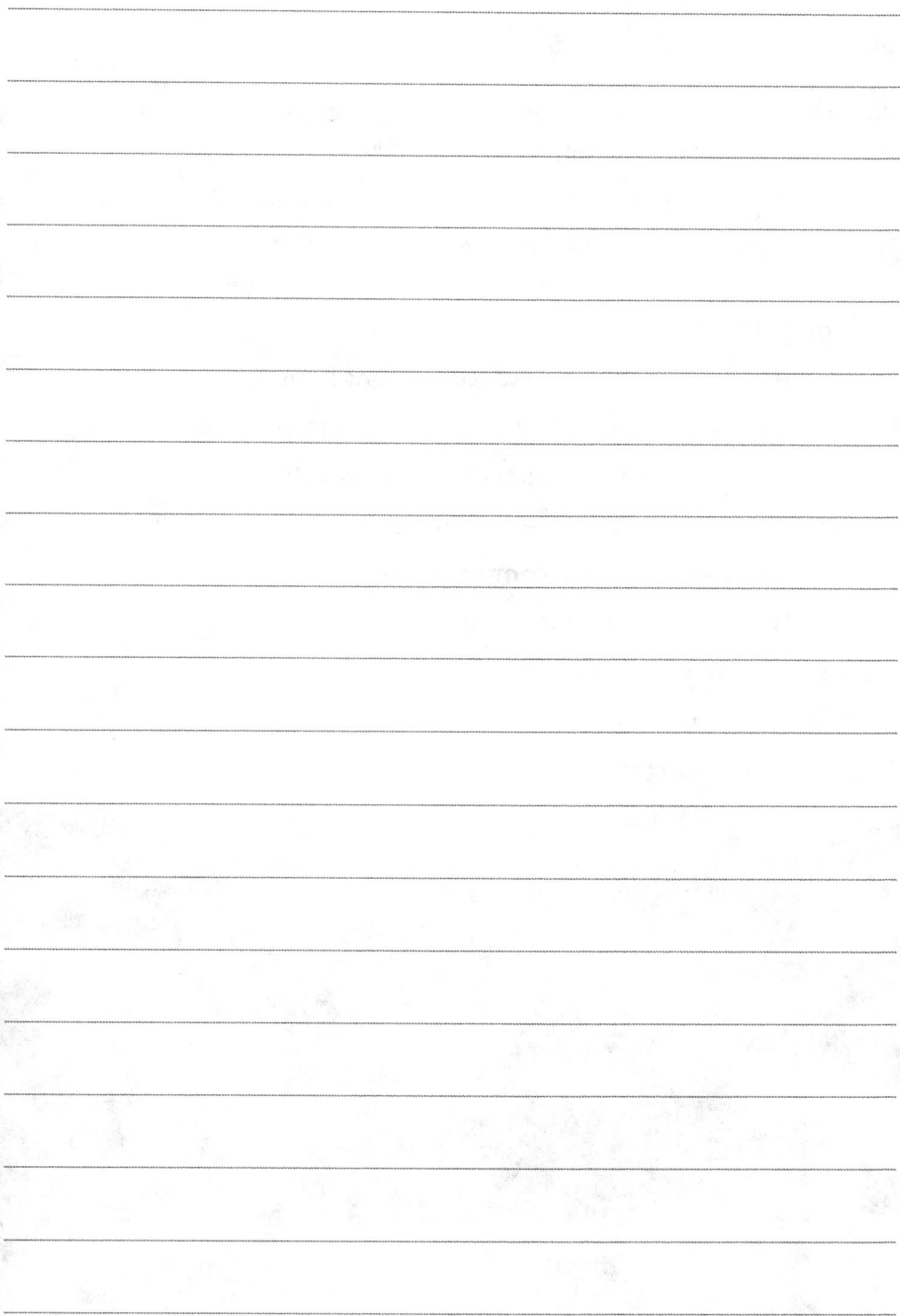

What Do You Think?

Here are some thoughts about playing with horses. What do you think they mean? How might they be true for you?

To err is human, but to blame the horse is even more human.

The horse doesn't care how much you know until he knows how much you care.

Can you get firm without getting mean or mad?

Find out what happens before what happens happens.

Prior and proper preparation prevents poor performance.

Passive persistence in the proper position pays off.

Take the time it takes so it takes less time.

Learning occurs outside the comfort zone.

Slow and right beats fast and wrong

Horses mirror our feelings.

Stop. Breathe. Think. Act.

Reward the slightest try.

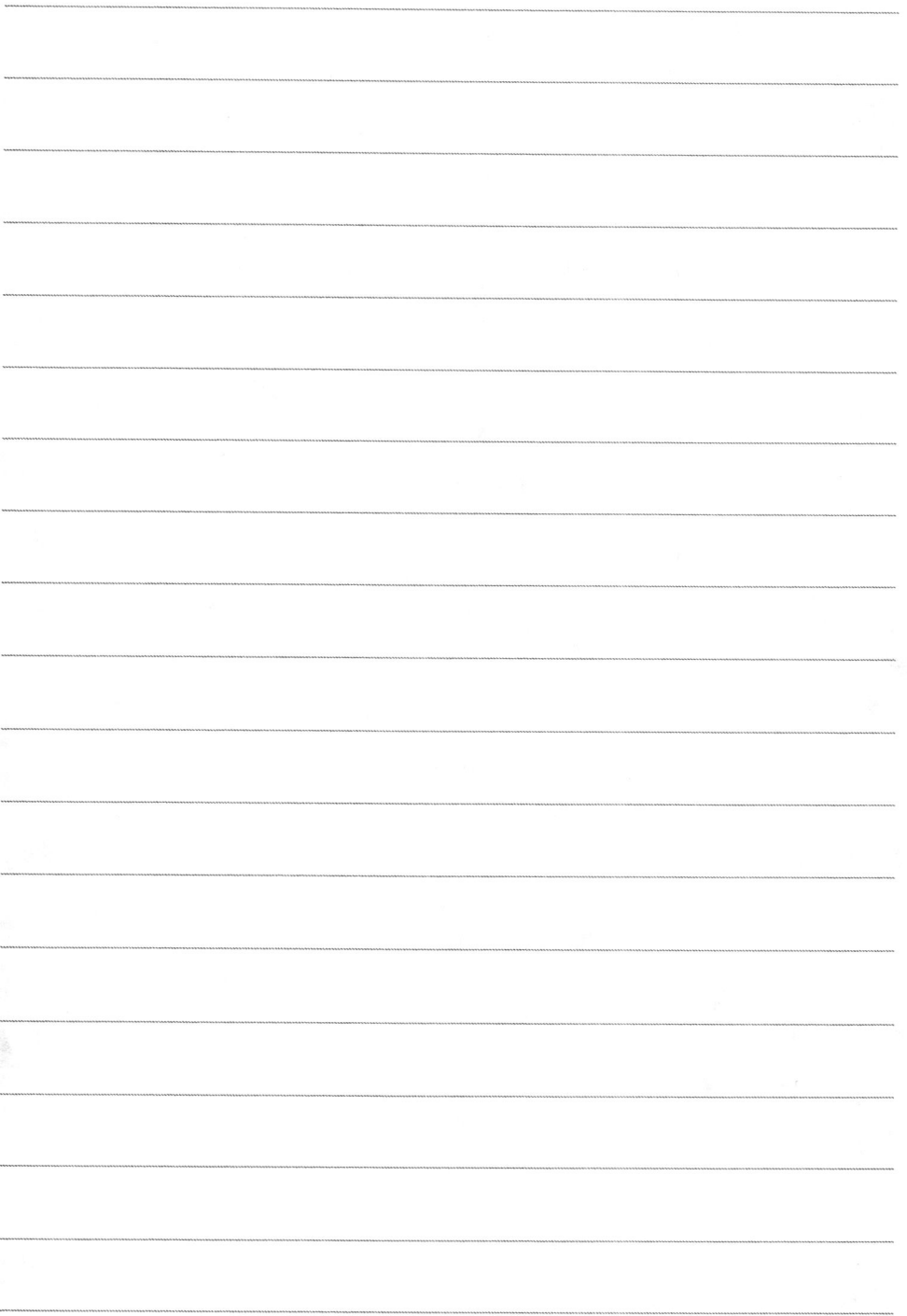

www.ingramcontent.com/pod-product-compliance
Lightning Source LLC
Chambersburg PA
CBHW050540280326
41933CB00011B/1659